Singing
OVER ME

Keep Singing!

DeSH

Rev. 21:4

A JOPLIN TORNADO
SURVIVOR'S JOURNEY

Singing
OVER ME

DANIELLE C. STAMMER

WestBow
PRESS
A DIVISION OF THOMAS NELSON

Unless otherwise noted, all Scripture taken from the Holy Bible,
New International Version®. Copyright © 1973, 1978, 1984 Biblica.
Used by permission of Zondervan. All rights reserved.

Scripture quotations in this publications are from The Message.
Copyright (c) by Eugene H. Peterson 1993, 1994, 1995, 1996, 2000,
2001, 2002. Used by permission of NavPress Publishing Group.

WestBow Press books may be ordered through booksellers or by contacting:

WestBow Press
A Division of Thomas Nelson
1663 Liberty Drive
Bloomington, IN 47403
www.westbowpress.com
1-(866) 928-1240

Because of the dynamic nature of the Internet, any web addresses or
links contained in this book may have changed since publication and
may no longer be valid. The views expressed in this work are solely those
of the author and do not necessarily reflect the views of the publisher,
and the publisher hereby disclaims any responsibility for them.

Any people depicted in stock imagery provided by Thinkstock are models,
and such images are being used for illustrative purposes only.

Certain stock imagery © Thinkstock.

ISBN: 978-1-4497-4830-2 (sc)
ISBN: 978-1-4497-4831-9 (hc)
ISBN: 978-1-4497-4829-6 (e)

Library of Congress Control Number: 2012906681

Printed in the United States of America

WestBow Press rev. date: 04/25/2012

To Andrew, my friend and love. When trials come, it's you I want by my side.

To Emily and Ethan. May you never give up and always know the Lord is with you.

To my Strong Lord Jesus. You are mighty to save, both in living and in life to come.

Foreword

We all have a need to make calamity intelligible, trying to fit what happens to us into the framework of what we think we already know about God and the way He relates to us and runs the world. But in this attempt and in all our losses we can miss the mercy of a Father who does not ever abandon His children nor loses control of the greater story. Ever. And we can miss the opportunity to both grieve and praise with holy intention. Danielle's personal story of surviving the Joplin, Missouri, tornado gives transparent testimony to what it means to truly lament, walking backward both through the debris and her own soul, finding that she and her family can live again. Open it quietly, let the words form pegs on which to hang your own losses and close it, more hopeful than when you began. I think Danielle's prayer is that you too will see a vision of the truth that in your worst moments, you were not alone and that the air was actually filled with singing.

Angela Blycker, author of *Running Into Water: Women Immersed in the Pursuit of God*

Preface

This book is my story, but my story is only one sentence in a whole book that could be entitled, The Joplin Tornado's Impact. I am writing for everyone who lost something on May 22nd and for those who are going through grief now. I am writing to encourage you to tell your story. It is unique, with its own, very personal losses and triumphs. I am writing in thanks and with awe to the flood of individuals who came to Joplin to serve and offer assistance. To the medical, public service and rescue workers; to the organizations and businesses who donated skills and supplies; to the churches and hospitals and colleges that received the overflow of homeless and hurting survivors; to the prayer warriors who cried out to the Lord on Joplin's behalf, even from miles away, thank you. Finally, I am writing to honor the Lord who walks with us, even through the valley of the shadow of death, thanking him for hope in loss, joy in grief and thankfulness in the midst of suffering.

Danielle C. Stammer

April 16, 2012

JOPLIN MISSOURI TORNADO PATH IMPACTED AREA

Legend

USACE - RFO

Structure Damage

Catastrophic Damage

Moderate Damage

Location Map

1. Heard sirens, turned around
2. Waited, calling friends, before hearing of cell forming just west
3. Stammer's house
4. St. John's Hospital

7th Street
20th Street
Indiana
26th Street
32nd Street
Freeman Hospital

Introduction

I t was stuck to my scalp, and no amount of washing was going to get it off today. I stood in a friend's shower and lathered up again. The grit on my head and in my ears was a mixture of dirt and debris that an EF-5 tornado had whipped onto me not even twenty-four hours ago. I wanted it off me.

I

Sunday, May 22nd

8:00 a.m.

Sunday, May 22, 2011, began like any other Sunday for Andrew and Danielle Stammer. Running late, they scrambled out the door for church and drove the twenty minutes north to Oronogo, Missouri. Later they met up with family for lunch before scurrying home to put down their two toddlers, Emily and Ethan, for their afternoon naps. This Sunday stood out because Danielle's parents and grandparents were in town for two celebrations: Andrew's graduation from nursing school and the birthday of Danielle's younger sister, Dalenna.

While the kids napped, the adults chatted about the weekend over coffee and cake. Dalenna and her boyfriend arrived later, and while everyone was saying good-bye, John kindly cleaned up the mess in the kitchen and washed the dishes. Then it was time to go. In the chaos of last-minute packing, somehow Diana, Danielle's mom, overlooked giving her first-born a hug and kiss good-bye. She realized it as the car was getting ready to pull out of the drive, and being the type who always seizes the day, she ran back inside to squeeze her daughter good-bye.

When the house was empty, Andrew and Danielle crashed on the couch, looked into each other's eyes, and breathed a sigh of relief and anticipation. The years of nursing school had been difficult, and tomorrow would begin a new season of life. Andrew had two weeks before starting a new position at St. John's Hospital, and the family was looking forward to rest and peace. They knew exactly what that looked like. The semester had afforded only a few nights for them to slip outside together, but those evenings were precious. While the sun had cast its magnificent spectrum of colors over them, Andrew and Danielle had worked together in their garden. They had watched their children playing on their swing set until darkness forced them inside. Monday would begin their season of rest. They would have to wait one more day.

Sunday night was small group night, so Danielle pulled herself off the couch and slipped into Emily's recently painted purple room. It was beautiful, and not just because her best friend, Cara, had done such a lovely job painting it for Emily's third birthday two weeks earlier. The room was glowing. It was a moment she knew she would never forget. The afternoon sun was illuminating the room with warmth and casting a pink glow over everything. Emily was still asleep, her long lashes closed, brushing against her round cheeks.

Danielle sat and stared. *It's easy to miss the beauty in the mundane, and it's so refreshing when it's appreciated.*

A thousand times before, fear whispering, "This is one of those last moments before something horrendous happens," tainted moments like this. But ironically, that thought did not come today. Something horrendous did happen, but it happened later. In this moment, no one had to feel its cold claws. It was a moment of grace because the family could later look back on the final scene of their story in that home and relive that glorious climax. They could have easily had a last moment of arguing or exasperation over childishness or defeat by the mess of daily life because all of these were parts of their story. Instead, serenity took the final bow.

Andrew came in with seventeen-month-old Ethan and sat by Danielle. Neither wanted to break the mood of the moment, but finally, the idea of being abysmally late urged them. They woke their daughter and dashed out the door.

2

One day after

Coming out of the shower that first afternoon, I was numb, robotic. So much had happened since last night. I had crashed into bed bruised and dirty, just trying to make it through the night. I fought demons in my sleep, seeing our survival over and over in my mind and replaying it, but changing one detail and fearing what could have been. I battled in my mind until the early hours of the morning when I declared truth the winner. We were alive. I knew the end of the story. So each time fear came knocking at my mind, I said to myself (and sometimes aloud), "We are alive."

We were alive but not together. I missed Andrew. I missed his strength. I wanted to collapse on him, letting him do all the work required of survivors. Andrew had been taken to a hospital in Kansas to be checked for injuries, which thankfully included only bruised ribs. His sister had met him there and taken him to her Kansas home to sleep that night. He was planning to come in their extra vehicle to be with us later that afternoon.

I had to stay strong that first morning. Our house was still standing but it was damaged. So before I could rest, heal, cry, or even take a shower, someone had to go to the house. Rain was supposed to come by nine in the morning, so early on the twenty-third, my father-in-law, Karl, and I quickly gathered some supplies from his garage and slowly picked our way through the debris-covered streets to my house.

My first impression on seeing the house was, "It isn't that bad."

Sure, I could see the sky from my living room, but had we been home when the storm struck, we would have been safe. Two young men with shock on their faces but purpose in their steps came walking up the street and asked if we needed any help. Together, Karl and I didn't have the strength to do what needed to be done, so we gratefully said yes.

All over Joplin, strangers were walking the streets lending help. Each of them realized they could do little to reverse the damage that had been done. It was in their eyes: awe at the destructive power of the wind mixed with steely resolve to do their part. The task was greater than any single willing person could handle, but multiplied thousands of times, those of us in need found help.

We needed to put tarps over the biggest holes in the roof, but we didn't have a ladder or much in the way of tools. Our shed that we had just cleaned and organized on Saturday had blown away, along with almost everything in it. Necessity really does give birth to invention, and I realized we could make this work. Part of our deck rail had splintered off, and we turned it on its side and made it into a ladder. Since we had no boards or nails, the two strangers found several concrete blocks to hold down the tarp. While they were working on the roof, I went through the house to assess the damage and to pack a few overnight bags to get us through the next few days. Dalenna, John, and John's dad also came over to help. The men affixed a piece of plywood over the smashed sliding glass door to prevent further damage to the house and, sadly, to keep out looters. Everything was looking up. Then it began to rain.

At first, we scrambled with buckets and bowls, trying to collect what we could. Dalenna and I diverted the large amount of water dripping onto my kitchen table by using a spare tarp to direct the streams outside, under the plywood covering my shattered back door.

It kept raining. The light fixture in the living room started gushing. In each room, we discovered the same: water pouring through the ceiling fixtures, finding the path of least resistance into my home. We moved bigger buckets under the heavier streams, but the rain kept coming. Dalenna and I tried desperately to move anything that was in the path of water. We opened Ethan's closet and realized we had forgotten about closet lights. Rain was pouring in over his toys and clothes. We pulled out everything as quickly as possible and looked for dry corners to stash heirlooms and precious gifts.

My room, the living room, and Emily's room had hardwood floors, which I loved. I started pulling my clothes out of the closet and used them as a mop in hopes of saving the floors. We kept cleaning, moving, drying, and dumping, and the rain kept coming. We pulled down every picture. The walls were starting to drip. Paint buckled under the streams of water seeping in, and I finally could do no more. Tears seeped out of the corners of my eyes and streamed down my face as I realized that, as hard as I had fought to save my home, I had lost.

3

Sunday, May 22nd

5:10 p.m.

On the drive north to their small group meeting, Danielle was holding a tray of tortilla chips and salsa. They were all hungry, so she started doling out chips. They were intended to be shared with their friends, so she only handed out a few. Those few would end up being their dinner. When they were a mile from their destination, they heard tornado sirens pierce the late afternoon air. Karl was their go-to weather person, so Andrew quickly called him.

"A cell capable of producing a tornado is moving toward the north side of Joplin," he said.

They turned the car around and drove a mile and a half back into Joplin. They parked to wait for the all clear and called Forrest and Jessica, their small group hosts, to warn them to take shelter and to explain where they were.

Forrest ended the conversation by saying, "Just call us later so we know you're okay."

"Andrew, I'm worried about Forrest and Jessica. I'm really nervous their house is going to be hit," Danielle confided. *It seems like tornados always circle to the north or south of Joplin. I really hope they're not taking this lightly,* she thought.

"I'm sure they'll take shelter and be fine," Andrew consoled. Then he added, "Make sure you call Cara, too."

Danielle hung up and called her best friend, Cara, and her husband, Eric, who lived north of Joplin, to warn them. While Andrew's phone rang, she tried to call Dalenna, who was shopping just a few blocks away from where they sat.

Karl had called back. "Another cell is forming west of Joplin around 7th Street, so just head to the hospital to take shelter. We'll meet you there."

Danielle's mind raced. *Whoa. That's almost straight west of where we're parked. Dalenna is right in its path. She needs to take shelter. I have to warn her.* While she called, Andrew quickly turned the car around and headed south, out of the predicted storm's path.

Some decisions are unforgettable. At that moment, Andrew decided to go home first to grab important documents and their laptops. Danielle sat in the car with their two children as the sky darkened overhead. A loud, cracking thump broke the quiet anxiousness. Then silence. Danielle whipped her head around, scanning to find the source of the noise, when another cracking thump hit. She saw hail, huge, intermittently falling chunks. She ran into the house, screamed at Andrew to come, and ran back to the car.

Andrew gave up the hunt for his backpack, which had caused his delay, took the wheel, turned left out of their driveway, and left again onto 26th Street, a straight shot to St. John's Hospital.

"Where are you going?" Danielle cried out in alarm, expecting him to drive south to 32nd Street and then to Freeman Hospital, but Andrew was an employee of St. John's, so his loyalties took him there.

"I'm going to St. John's," came his determined reply.

"Does St. John's have a shelter tunnel, too? Aren't your parents meeting us at Freeman?"

"It does, and I'll call my parents, but I think they're headed here, too."

Still thinking the storm was moving north of them, Danielle tried to keep her sister safe. Dalenna texted that she was in the backroom of the store, hunkered down. Danielle tried to call, but only got Dalenna's voice mail. She put her phone in the middle console and looked up as their van drove the path the tornado would soon take and into a sky as black as night.

4

Sunday, May 22ⁿᵈ

6:00 p.m.

Dalenna, Eric, Cara, Forrest, and Jessica would
soon hear about the monster that ripped across
Joplin, and all five of them would wonder if Andrew
and Danielle were still alive. Forrest and Jessica would
drive as far as they could into Joplin and walk over
two and a half miles to the Stammer's empty house.
Upon realizing it was empty, they would spray an "X"
on the garage door to signify the house was checked for

survivors and continue down the block, checking each home and marking it accordingly.

Dalenna would drive a different path, getting there first and leaving only moments before another couple arrived. They had narrowly survived by lying on the ground in a nearby parking lot and had walked to the Stammer's house to look for refuge.

Eric and Cara would watch the sky darken and quickly clear up from their home north of Joplin. Thinking the scare had come and gone, they would head out for dinner and hear the disturbing news there. As they listened for more information, they heard the updated reports asking people to keep clear of the affected area. They would drive as close as they could to transport friends who'd been caught in the path, while praying for others as they waited for news.

Danielle's parents, Dale and Diana, were ten minutes from home on their three-hour drive back to Jefferson City when Dale's sister called.

"Hello, Marsha! How are you?" came Diana's pleasant surprise at Marsha's call.

"I can tell from your voice that you don't know what's going on."

Immediately, Diana assumed something had happened to one of her husband's siblings or maybe his mom. *Dale's mom is eighty. What happened to her?* She grasped for ideas.

"A bad tornado in Joplin hit St. John's Hospital," spilled out the rest of Marsha's words.

We were just in Joplin three hours ago. St. John's is only a mile and a half from the house. Diana's thoughts franticly swarmed. *If the tornado were big enough to cause damage to a huge hospital, were the kids hurt?*

"We'll call the girls," Diana said, "and find out what's going on and let you know."

Diana turned to Dale, "Joplin was hit by a large tornado. We need to go back."

"Let's get more information first. Call the girls. If we are going back, I have supplies at home that'll be useful."

Diana resisted. "Turn around."

"No, let's go home and get some supplies," Dale protested.

"Turn around now. We're going back!" Diana was not one to make demands on her husband, but she was so adamant that Dale reluctantly obliged.

As they drove, Diana called every phone number that would reach a loved one, but none of their calls to Joplin were connecting. They couldn't make contact. The lack of information was making them uneasy.

Diana's mom called next. "Did you hear there was a tornado in Joplin?"

"Marsha just called. We were almost home, but we're heading back now."

"You better. What about Danielle and Dalenna?"

"I can't get through to the girls."

"Diana, it looks bad. The news is awful. Oh, my goodness…Oh my…I'm watching the news right now. We were all just there. Everything is destroyed. It looks like the tornado went from one side of the city to the other." As she related what had been on the news concerning the size and scope of the damage, their hearts sank.

They kicked into overdrive and sped back toward Joplin with flashers on, warning other drivers to keep a safe distance. More news came in. I-44 was blocked off just outside of Joplin. Semis had been blown over, blocking the road now covered in debris. This was huge. The devastation was more than they could imagine, and with the road blocked, they wouldn't be able to get there that night. Dale called a friend and asked him to find them a hotel as close to Joplin as he could.

The phone rang. It was Dalenna! She had gotten through. Diana answered the call quickly, "Dalenna! Are you okay?"

"I'm fine. I wasn't in the path of the storm. My apartment is okay too, but there's no power."

"Marsha called and told us about the tornado. We were ten minutes from home, but we turned around. We're on our way there right now. Have you heard from Danielle?"

"They're not at the house. We just left from there. It's mostly okay. The roof is damaged. Danielle left me a voice message saying they were going to St. John's."

"St. John's! That was on the news. The tornado hit there!"

"Mama, don't worry. There's a shelter there, and Danielle's message said they were going to the shelter. They'll be fine."

Despite Dalenna's reassurances, doubt remained. St. John's had been directly hit. Dale and Diana were certain they were driving to Joplin for a funeral. Diana remembered she had almost forgotten to give her daughter a hug good-bye, but the hug she gave wasn't intended to be a final good-bye. The memory was of little comfort.

Two bars. One bar. Blinking battery icons. As more news came in, both spirits and batteries sank critically low. With no more expectation of getting to Joplin that night, they stopped at a fast-food restaurant to charge their cells in the slimmest hope that good news would come. No one in the almost-vacant restaurant knew what had happened, but within moments, TVs came to life. Everyone inside gave of themselves to help Dale and Diana. Food was offered for free. Anyone with Internet on their phone was trying to find a back road route that would get the worried parents to Joplin. The immediate willingness to assist was a spirit that would show itself again and again over the next several months as people from around the nation and even the world would selflessly do whatever they could for this battered community. In the end, it was determined that all roads to Joplin were blocked and the anxious couple could only wait and pray, getting as close to their destination as permitted. Worried, isolated, and helpless, they checked into a hotel.

5

Two days after

On the morning of May 24, I woke up next to my bruised husband and said, "Happy eighth anniversary." And oddly enough, it was a happy anniversary. We had no candlelight dinner, no fancy moments of poetic reflection, or no spoiling of any kind, but we were together.

The reality of our losses was still before us. We met friends at our house that morning and packed up everything we could save and loaded it into a trailer. Insulation was covering the floor in the living room where the ceiling had fallen during the night, giving way to the wet weight saturating it. It made a mess, but we worked around it and saved what we could.

It was humbling to see how many people were immediately available to help us. Our friends from different circles had come together, united around their common care for us. While we were working, the ceiling in the dining room fell, peppering our table with insulation, but no one was hurt. The work continued until we had gotten everything we could hold.

I remember the house feeling quiet despite the number of people in it. Except for necessary working conversation, no one spoke. We were all in awe of what we were doing and seeing and living through. Destruction was all around us; salvage was now the goal.

The hard question came, "Do you want to save this?"

Of course. It's mine. I had it here, didn't I? I guess it's not important. It's damaged now; it's useless. The words in my head stayed there, and maybe the emotion of the decision played on my face, but my words never betrayed me as I calmly answered, "No."

It's odd to pack up your entire home in a morning, sorting things by wet or dry instead of by bedroom and kitchen and using trash bags for laundry and plastic storage containers instead of boxes. I was so thankful John had done the dishes the previous afternoon. They could be packed quickly today.

A rose in a vase was sitting on the bookshelf that divided the dining room from the living room. Four evenings before, that rose had been given to Andrew during his pinning ceremony, part of his graduation from nursing school. My husband loves me, and that night, he wanted everyone else to know it. After he walked across the stage to accept his rose, he unceremoniously walked out of line to where I was sitting to give it to me in thanks for all my support of him while he was studying. It made me smile just thinking about it.

The rose was now in full bloom, which was in stark contrast to the exposed ceiling beams, bleeding insulation, framed behind it. It spoke of beauty in chaos and love in turmoil. As everyone filtered out of the house to load up the last few things, Andrew and I slipped into our empty bedroom and danced, humming the song we danced to on our wedding day eight years earlier.

6

Sunday, May 22nd

5:30 p.m.

While driving into the darkness, Danielle realized that this could turn into a bad situation at any moment, so she voiced her fears in prayer, "Lord, please watch over our family. We need your help."

As they crested the small hill leading to St. John's, they could see transformers exploding as white, hot light sliced through the ominous blackness at the intersection in front of them.

"Go to Freeman!" Danielle shouted in desperation.

"No," Andrew replied quickly. "There's no time. We're here."

Andrew rounded the corner, pulled up directly beside the hospital's eastern basement entrance, and parked under the awning of a glass entryway.

"Are you going to park here?" Danielle asked in alarm, thinking of all the people who would be coming in after them and all the people who would need to get out after the tornado scare was over.

"Yes, I'm going to park here," Andrew firmly replied. He knew there wasn't much time now.

Danielle jumped out of the car, slid the tray of chips onto the dash, and left the laptops and documents on her seat. She intended to get Ethan inside and then quickly return for a second load. The air was sticky, quiet, and calm, but her heart raced as adrenaline sharpened her senses. She reached for the door, but it was still locked. Andrew looked up in alarm as Danielle's wedding ring rapped hard on the glass. He quickly hit the unlock button. The rear sliding doors opened in unison as both parents reached for their children, and the wind began to circle through their van.

Still not aware of the magnitude of the danger swirling around them, Danielle calmly and quickly unfastened Ethan's seat beat. "It's windy, baby," she soothed as she scooped him up, closed the door, and briskly walked inside the glass enclosure.

Once inside, she turned around and immediately realized she would not be taking a second trip to the car. After pulling his barefoot little girl out of the car and up to his chest, Andrew went around the front of the van. The wind had gotten strong fast. Danielle watched him hunched over, struggling against the wind to get to safety, only to realize safety wasn't safe.

As soon as they were all together, they looked around. They were standing in open air in the middle of a semicircle of windows leading to the hospital's entrance. The sliding glass door that usually opened welcomingly was closed tight. The hospital had been locked down for protection. No one in and no one out. Panic clouded Danielle's mind as she scanned the room, looking for anywhere to protect her babies from the glass that would soon give way to the wind's pressure. Everything was quiet in her mind because the storm had reached deafening screams. It was only as she turned toward Andrew that she realized he had found a solution. It wasn't likely to work, but it was something to try in desperation. Still holding Emily to his chest, Andrew was systematically ramming his shoulder into the sliding door, attempting to force an entrance.

In this moment, a hero emerged. Heroes come in different sizes and shapes. Andrew is neither a powerful muscle man nor athletic professional. He's a man committed to his family. He doesn't spend his time lifting weights in the gym, but instead, he bench-presses his children as they play together on the floor. He doesn't wrestle giants, just toddlers over bedtimes. He doesn't chase trophies, just children around the house. Andrew is a man of passion, persistence, and conviction.

Faced against all odds, Andrew did not give up. He did not hesitate. He did not even feel pain. He fought. He strained. He won. In a few moments, the storm would shatter the glass that was holding up to Andrew's pressure, but before it could, the door was forced off its lower track. Andrew had done it. He rescued their family. Danielle realized their opportunity and yelled for Andrew to slip through it. He couldn't hear her over the wind, but at her second attempt, he saw what she was indicating and slipped through the crack between the door and the frame. Danielle quickly followed as the tornado hit St. John's with full force and the lights went out.

7

Two days after

The unthinkable had happened. Joplin had been slit across the midsection, and it was still bleeding. I felt exposed and raw. The tornado had been unrelenting, and the rain came as salt on a wound.

Then came the updated warnings. "Severe weather alert. Storms capable of producing tornados tonight." My senses were numb, but I felt the worst was possible. We were going to be hit again. The path was already made, inviting new terrors to spin down it. How could I think otherwise? The worst-case scenario two evenings ago was now a historical reality.

"Just come and stay with us for a bit," my parents pleaded.

"Let's get you out of here for now."

"The children can't be allowed to see all this."

"You'll be safe in Jefferson City. Tornados don't hit Jeff because it's close to the Missouri River and because of all the hills."

It felt right. I wanted to be as far away from tornado warnings as possible. My heart raced at the thought of the sirens blaring again. I was jittery inside, so we left to stay with my parents for a few days.

That first evening in Jefferson City, I drew a bath for my children. They love "tubby time," so it was a joy to give them something familiar in a familiar place. Yet, my heart pulled inside me as I placed their scratched and bruised bodies into the warm water. They played like always, but it was hard to watch them. *They're safe but not safe enough. It was too close. Kids shouldn't have to go through things like this.*

The nights were already getting easier. I could close my eyes without seeing the dark wind howling around us. Speaking out the truth that first night helped me escape the trauma of reliving my trauma in my dreams, but during the day, I was not spared. It was spring, and stormy weather followed us.

Only three days ago, on Sunday, I sat around my dining room table with my family enjoying the day, and now I was sitting in my parents' kitchen getting ready to eat a home-cooked meal my Aunt Marsha and my grandma had made for us. So much had changed so fast, and they knew we were exhausted. Although food is essential to life, it's hard to make it a priority in seasons of loss. Bringing a meal to a hurting, exhausted family is a simple and profound blessing.

As we sat down together to thank the Lord and begin the meal, sirens interrupted us. I couldn't believe it. My insides were panicking while I fought to be calm. *Oh no. Not again. Are they following us? Like Jonah, has trouble come to the whole ship because we are on it?*

They were silly questions. They were selfish questions as if we were the cause of the weather, but they were real questions. The answer is no. It was a stormy season. It had nothing to do with us.

We quietly headed to the basement, masking the reality of the situation by building tents for the kids to play under in the safest corner. I could see the upper floors being ripped away in my imagination, but that was only my mind's eye. We were spared. A tornado did hit Sedalia, Missouri, that afternoon, and more Missouri families were affected.

The strength of my reaction to the sirens made me realize that healing wouldn't come in a blink or by placing myself in a safer situation. I was afraid of what I had already survived.

Survival was what we fought for and what we were relieved to attain. Several times, though, during that first week, I found myself thinking, with desire in my heart, about how close I had come to entering God's glory. I could almost hear the sounds of heavenly worship. I could almost feel its tangible peace. My heart swelled when I imagined myself finally getting to see my Lord Jesus face-to-face. Not yet. It was difficult to accept, as if I had a choice.

I know a day will come, somewhere on the path, when my desires will be realized. The fullness of my experiences in this life will fade out of focus, and what I have only longed for will sharpen in clarity. On that day, my joy will be complete, and I will see the true reality of my life as I worship my King.

8

Sunday, May 22nd

Approximately 5:40 p.m.

As soon as Danielle and Ethan squeezed through the door, the lights went out, and they were flung down on the floor. Where hospital patrons usually stood waiting for the elevator, Danielle hit the ground hard. The weight of Ethan's body caused the brunt of her fall to land on her forearms, which were still wrapped tightly around her little boy. Her left hand cradled his head, protecting it from hitting the floor, but he still felt the impact. He started to cry.

While the wind was screaming around her, shattering windows, ripping off roofs, tossing cars in a heap, and shredding mature trees to the size of toothpicks, she began to sing. Calming her baby. Calming herself. Worshipping the Creator it seemed she was about to meet. Her mind was clear as she sang and asked God to protect Andrew and Emily, not knowing what had happened to them. The glass that had barred their entrance only moments before was now raining down on her back, finding its way under her clothes. And then, a thought pierced her mind. *I'm still alive. We have to move.*

She struggled to her feet, hunched over, and sloshed her way through debris in flip-flops until she found the open door to the stairwell just past the elevator.

Later, she would come back to this spot and see the miracle of her survival. A chunk of concrete would be resting on the floor where she and Ethan had been flung. *Could it be that it came to rest there only moments after we moved? Why hadn't more debris fallen on us?* The answer was seen in the aftermath. A florescent light box had been dislodged from the entryway ceiling and came to rest on what used to be someone's mattress. The wind had wedged them against the windows, like a shield protecting her and

Ethan from dangerous debris. They had been spared, but for now, the storm was still raging.

The worst of it had passed the hospital, leaving it battered, broken, and dislodged from its foundation by four inches. As Danielle entered the stairwell, she saw the exit door had blown open, and the powerful after-wind was still blowing debris around outside. Crawling as close as possible to the wall pocketed by the base of the stairs, Danielle and Ethan huddled. Ethan was no longer crying. In fact, he was very quiet. He held to Danielle and waited. As another song came and with it more prayers for Andrew and Emily, it was still hard to hear herself over the roar outside. She sat for what seemed like a long time, wondering and waiting.

9

June

A month and several trips back to Joplin later, I was finally looking forward to something again. Andrew and I were going on a date. We were leaving in a couple days for a weekend away with our friends, Eric and Cara. In the last month, we had rearranged my parents' house to accommodate four additional people. We had sorted through our possessions, cleaning and packing up most of them, leaving things with friends, or hauling them up to Jefferson City. Then there was the paperwork. The fact there was no Internet capability at my parents' house complicated all of the paperwork we had to submit to multiple disaster relief organizations and our insurance company. We scraped out time to run to coffee shops or the library in order to keep the processes moving.

On trips to Joplin, we utilized work teams of volunteers to clean up the mess our house now was. One day, a large group of workers pulled out all the soggy walls, electric lines, cabinets, and floors. I was glad I didn't have to watch the wood floors I enjoyed so much heading to the trash heap or see Emily's pretty purple walls come down. It had to be done. Sometimes tearing down is a part of rebuilding, even though it stings like antiseptic on a wound. I was thankful that Andrew could be strong for me and do what was needed then, but being thankful was a struggle.

On June 21, 2011, my journal recorded:

> *Father, I feel layers of unhealed stresses on me. How can I heal when new ones keep coming? Being displaced and all that goes with that was a blow we never expected. I'm so afraid I'll never heal, that something else is coming next, before I have time to recover. I have two reactions: fear I'll crumble and a hardened resolve that we'll survive. The "bring it on" reaction has a*

bit of cynicism to it and no heart. I waver between
these two every day, but I feel your spirit nudging me
to take a different look at it all. Thankfulness. I am
so thankful to have so many people helping me. I'm
thankful my parents have such a large home and large
hearts to accommodate us. I'm thankful that Andrew
has finished school and has a profession that travels
well. I'm thankful that I'm married to a strong and
sensible man who protects his family. I'm thankful
that your spirit guides us, teaches us, and heals us. I'm
thankful that our injuries from the tornado were minor
and we could save most of our things. And mostly, I'm
thankful for the assurance that, had the storm taken
our lives, it would have taken us into your loving arms
and no other.

The weekend finally came. Andrew and I drove to
the scenic campground where we would meet Eric and
Cara. The drive gave us time to talk and relax. We went
on a hike that overlooked a beautiful spring. We shared
a tasty meal and spent the evening playing games and
laughing with our friends, but in the quiet, my thoughts
came alive. While everyone else was napping the next
afternoon, I grabbed my journal and began to write.

June has flown by, almost in a blink. I feel in some ways that I missed it or was in a fog, and in some ways, that's true. But now, right now, it's quiet and still.

Quiet has a way of wrenching out what we stuff inside. As I sat in stillness, I realized some lurking thoughts.

I have some sore spots from the aftermath of the tornado that haven't healed, and most deal with my relationship with Andrew. I really can't pinpoint all of them, but I notice things aren't right because small offenses are oozing like infected wounds, hurting much deeper than they should.

There had been a lot of business to do in the last month, and traditionally, I'm pretty good at living in business mode, but when I do, the people around me suffer. I'm not soft and gentle because the highest priority becomes completing a task and people often get in the way of tasks. I knew I couldn't blame all my sharpness and lack of patience on the workload. Something else was eating at me, and I found myself snapping and snarling at Andrew for reasons even I didn't understand until I sat long enough to think and write, probing the pain inside me.

While I'm writing this, my mind keeps flashing back to the conversation Andrew and I had right before the tornado hit. I was so mad at Andrew for putting us in a compromising situation. I remember saying to him on the drive to St. John's, "It's more important to be alive than it is to be dead with our laptops and important documents with us." I lost some respect, trust, or something with Andrew that night. His job was to protect us (not ultimately, of course, because, even in the midst of Andrew's mistakes, God protected us), but he made compromising decisions that put us in danger.

I realized what I was doing. Because I didn't trust him to do what was best for us, I began to operate our relationship on new terms.

I feel like I have to take over and make all the decisions. I hate that. I want to rest under his leadership, trust his wisdom, and operate as a team again.

I'm learning that it's a discipline to see the good in people and situations, but it's also the only way to heal. Philippians 4:8 tells me that I do best by filling my mind and meditating on things true, noble, reputable, authentic, compelling, and gracious. The best, not the worst. The beautiful, not the ugly. Things to praise, not to curse (The Message). In every situation, there are both ugly and beautiful things. I often see the ugly. I think most of us do. When our minds are stuck on the negative, our bodies hold those emotions as poison inside us, and we become slaves to our pain. In my journal, I realized I had a lot to be thankful for. Andrew is not a quitter. He's a fighter, and he's strong.

> *At St. John's, Andrew did what I could not have done for our family. He got us to safety through his strength and insight. And in the end, we were okay.*

It was time for me to talk to Andrew. He needed to know I forgave him and I was willing to rebuild a trusting relationship with him. It was time to do what is so difficult for me. I needed to ask forgiveness for my bitterness and pride.

I was looking forward to this weekend vacation because I wanted a break, but what I gained was better: insight into myself and the beginnings of reconciliation with my husband.

On our last morning of escape, we got a phone call. Our sister-in-law's father had passed away that morning. The funeral would be Wednesday … in Joplin.

10

Sunday, May 22ⁿᵈ

Approximately 5:40 p.m.

For Andrew and Emily, breaking into the hospital did not guarantee safety. As they slipped through the broken door, the tornado hit full force, and all the lights went out. In a groping search for a safe corner, Andrew unknowingly struggled forward into a wind tunnel circulating through the building.

On a normal day at St. John's, had Andrew used the east entrance to come to work as a student nurse tech, he would have walked through the sliding glass door and either taken the elevator to his immediate right or the stairs to the left of the elevator. Today, he saw the alcove at the base of the stairs before the lights went out and headed toward them. At that moment, the winds ripped open the exit door and circled through the building. Andrew was caught in its path and immediately lost control of his destiny.

His six-foot-four, 230-pound frame was lifted from behind like a feather, and he flew with three-year-old Emily, still in a bear hug to his chest, toward the exterior door. His legs spun like a tire stuck in mud in hopes of finding contact with the floor, but he could not control his movement. He was heading toward the exit and out into the heart of the storm.

Luck is something to which the superstitious attribute their destiny. It could be said that Andrew is a lucky man. In fact, Andrew himself would later think back on this day and concede he was lucky, but Andrew is also a man of faith. He knows that God is the final author of our stories, and in that moment heading toward death, Andrew instead slammed into the door frame and somehow found himself crumpled outside at the base of the stairwell leading up to the main level parking lot. He was on the bottom stair with Emily safely tucked under him. One hand gripped the stair rail, and the other clung to his frightened daughter. It was here they waited. Prayed. Waited.

Not knowing where Danielle and Ethan were, Andrew prayed. He felt guilty. *Why did I slip through the door first? I should have made sure Danielle was safely inside before following. I'm stronger than she is.* He roared as if he had to overcome the noise in order to be heard. *"Please help us, God!"*

Above them, the storm raged while the railing around the perimeter of the stairs caught debris, protecting them from further harm. When the wind finally passed over them and a cold calm settled, Andrew stood up, still holding Emily, and resolved himself to find his wife and son. He ducked back through the door frame, which had painfully saved his life, and to his immediate relief, he saw Danielle and Ethan huddled in the corner to his right. They were all alive. Instead of basking in the joy of their survival, though, Danielle was frantic to find a better place to hide in case a second tornado followed. Into the broken hospital their family climbed.

Danielle and Andrew, Easter 2011

Emily, Easter 2011

Ethan, Easter 2011

Retrieving belongings from our van at the hospital's East entrance

Debris-filled East entrance (door Andrew broke on far left)

Protective shield of debris
for Danielle and Ethan

Andrew and Emily
waited out the storm at
the base of these steps

Stammer's backyard, including innovative "ladder"

Above: Karl
with his parents,
Verona and Don

Right: Emily seeing
her "broken house"
for the first time,
September 2011

II

July

When we saw Andrew's brother and grieving wife at the funeral, our embraces were more than just hellos. Living two states away meant we hadn't seen each other since before the tornado almost took our lives, and in a place of grief and mourning, there was a measure of joy. We stayed an extra day to be with them and then rushed back to Jefferson City for our garage sale.

I love garage sales. I love going to them, and I love having them. All throughout the year, I pile up items we grow out of or don't need in preparation for a sale. I was ready to have another sale when the tornado forced our move, and because all the items in our garage were spared, we decided to have our sale in Jefferson City. We needed space in the house.

On Friday, we had a little bit of success, but we really needed everything gone. We had a name-your-price sale, hoping people would take anything they could use. And then we were surprised. The local newspaper was tipped about a sale for a Joplin family where all prices were accepted, and they came to interview us. On Saturday, the story printed, and a steady stream of people came and lavished us with absurd generosity.

"Will you take $50 for a bottle of water?"

"How about $100 for these pants?"

"Here's a check for $500. I don't need anything."

The sense of community and love we felt overwhelmed us. Jefferson City's community was strong, and wherever we went, we found people who could help us be strong, too. Our church immediately embraced us, and we began to feel at home.

Every time we traveled to Joplin, though, I felt like I was coming home. I was around people who understood what we felt. I could witness renewal happening, and I was sad we were rebuilding our lives so far away. On the other hand, I felt such deep sadness, especially when we drove familiar roads that no longer looked familiar. I would hear myself saying in my head the words I said aloud only months before.

"Look! There's the high school!"

"Emily, what street do we live on?"

Looking now revealed only a heap of brick and twisted metal, and our street was no longer where we called home. Every time we came back to Joplin, I felt torn. Being in Jefferson City felt right for our family, but when we were back in Joplin, that felt right, too. I realized my heart was really in two places.

We had to make a decision, especially regarding work for Andrew. He was looking for work in Jefferson City, but nothing was available. He looked for work thirty miles away in Columbia, which seemed promising. Then on a whim, he applied at Freeman Hospital in Joplin, and he was immediately accepted for a position. I was stunned, and panic rose in my chest. That answered the job question, but it raised a lot of others. Where would we live? Is that good for our family? What do our children need right now? In the end, it was simply too much and too soon. We weren't ready to jump back in when we had a comfortable, familiar, and safe place to heal in Jefferson City. I felt guilty not fighting for

Joplin and being committed to rebuilding, but my guilt wasn't enough of a motivation to put my family through more unknowns.

A week after our sale, my mom and I, along with my children, were once again in the car on the way to Joplin. I was weary from traveling, but this trip was important. My little sister was having a bridal shower. Here again was rejoicing in a season of trials. John had planned to propose on Dalenna's birthday, but that was the day after the tornado. Instead of a proposal, they were at the house with me fighting the rain. He did propose the weekend after, and a September wedding was planned.

Our trip was quick and busy, and I wanted to see more people than I was able to. We hadn't been able to visit Andrew's grandparents yet and give them the hugs of survivors. I planned to drive the forty miles to see them that weekend with Andrew's mom, Pamela, but she got sick that afternoon, so the trip was cancelled. Grandpa and Grandma had been on my mind. I dropped them a letter in the mail on Saturday. *Maybe next time*, I thought.

Sunday was another three-hour drive back to Jefferson City. I was relieved to see the house as we drove up the street, knowing Andrew was there to greet me.

I was tired of traveling, making decisions, and seeing reminders of our losses, and I was glad to be home. We trooped in the house, and while we were still greeting each other, Andrew's phone rang. It was his dad.

He slipped out of sight and came back a moment later with a shocked look on his face. "Grandma and Grandpa were killed in a car accident today."

We crumpled to the floor and sobbed. I cried for myself, and I cried for Andrew. I cried for the letter they'd never receive, the missed chance to say good-bye, and grief upon grief. How could we lose more right now? How could I go on when the road is so hard? Would we ever heal? Would we ever rest?

12

Sunday, May 22nd

Approximately 5:45 p.m.

St. John's was indeed broken. Debris clung to all surfaces, dripping from window frames and piling on the floor. Debris is an interesting word. It's perfect to describe all the mess after a storm, but it's a sad word. Debris is what used to be progress, business, home, or memories. Pieces that were evidence of life, success, and civilization are now images of death, destruction, and loss. Andrew and Danielle sloshed their way into a cave of debris, still carrying their children, and saw a light bobbing in the distance coming toward them. A stunned hospital worker picked his way over. He looked dazed, but dutifully asked, "You guys okay?"

"I think so," Danielle replied.

"Follow me, and I'll take you to what we're using as an emergency room."

Despite all the destruction around them, Danielle couldn't grasp what had happened to the hospital. In her mind, the broken glass and debris around them were the only damage the hospital sustained. She knew they had caused some of the damage and feeling the need to confess, blurted into the silence, "We broke a door down."

The man ignored her honest confession and silently led them down the hallway. As they walked, Danielle tried again, "Sir, we actually broke one of the doors trying to get inside."

The man continued to walk without reply. Seeing his wife's utter confusion, Andrew, who better realized the scope of damage St. John's had sustained, spoke up, "Honey, I think they have bigger problems right now."

The makeshift emergency room was dark except for a single light coming in from an adjacent room. Dazed people sat around the perimeter, and the Stammers took their place. Danielle attempted to sit down, but her pants had collected glass, which crunched as she bent. She handed Ethan to Andrew and slipped into the bathroom in the corner. There she turned out her pants and heard the pieces tinkle on the floor. When she came back to Andrew, there were rumors of someone in need close by.

Not realizing Andrew was hurt, Danielle encouraged, "Andrew, why don't you go help? You're a nurse now."

He reluctantly, but dutifully agreed and handed her the children. She sat down, held them close, and sang in their ears.

A younger woman, blond highlighted hair pulled back into a quick ponytail, stood nearby, praying aloud. She was obviously distressed and still nervous, but before any connection was made, a nurse came in and ordered everyone to follow. Danielle didn't know where Andrew was or how he would be able to find them again. They all trudged out of the room in line, turning several corners until they were lost in the maze. People were hysterical and irrational, vying for attention and a chance to tell what had just happened to them. No one could listen. Instead, hospital staff quickly checked and mentally sorted people, looking for those with critical needs first.

Danielle stood quietly and looked in a room across the hall. A large and expensive testing machine sat there with water dripping on it and collecting on the floor. St. John's had just remodeled their computer systems and updated other areas to serve their patients better. They were a good company, and Andrew was proud to work with them. It seemed senseless for them to lose everything right now.

⸺

Andrew did what he could, but he struggled. He was in pain, triggering his head to swim and his eyes to fade out of focus. He also knew he needed to be with his family. He followed the line of people until he caught up with them. Joyous relief was on Danielle's face when she saw him, but Andrew looked troubled. Something was weighing heavily on his heart.

Andrew still had his cell phone, but no calls would connect. "I'm trying to get in touch with my parents, but the calls won't won't go through."

In reply, Danielle searched her pockets and realized she must have left hers in the car. Neither phone would have been able to connect. The towers were down.

With a twisted face, Andrew confided to Danielle his fear, "While you were trying to call Dalenna, my dad called me. They were on their way here, and he told me, 'Just get to safety. It's too late for us.' I think they're gone."

Danielle's mind raced. *Gone? No. It can't be. I can't imagine them gone, but if they were driving here it's not likely they made it. No. I refuse to let myself grieve on assumptions. We have to know first. Maybe, just maybe, they made it.*

A new order came from one of the nurses taking charge. "If you are not injured, come this way. If you are, stay."

Andrew needed to stay, so as Danielle struggled to lift both of her barefoot children, the woman who had been praying aloud in the first room came over and offered to hold Emily. Emily was hesitant, but obliged when Danielle coaxed her. "This nice lady is going to hold you, but you'll be right by mommy."

"I'm Christal."

"Thank you, Christal. I'm Danielle. This is Emily. I really appreciate you helping me. I wasn't sure how I was going to manage with both of them."

The uninjured were stuffed into a small hallway where power lines were exposed and the ceiling was collapsing. To Danielle's numb relief, Christal kept a sharp eye out for possible dangers. The emergency lights blinked, overly bright and inconsistent. The lights, the damp, the panic lurking just below mildly brave exteriors: *Is this real?* It seemed like a scene from a movie where war-beaten, battered and disheveled characters hide in a treacherous location as they struggle for survival. A ceiling piece teetered and threatened to give way over a young man's head. Christal saw it. Another man was tall enough to remove it safely. Momentary victory lapsed into more nervous waiting. Cramped. Uneasy. Still the lights flashed. *I just want to get out of here. No. Stay calm. Be patient.* Ethan's thirty pounds were getting heavier and Danielle's arms began to ache. Finally, another nurse announced it was time to move out. Firemen were coming to lead the way.

Instead of stepping out of darkness and into light, their first glimpse of the outside was a drizzly gray sky weeping over a war zone scene.

"Don't look, baby," came Christal's motherly concern to Emily.

Cars were scattered and stacked, buildings were in rubble, light poles were bent over, and the worst of it, there were no trees. There was nothing familiar left to use for a point of orientation. Only a look back at the hospital's emergency room sign would tell where they were.

A young woman with a strong voice ordered, "Get as far away from the hospital as possible. There's a gas leak."

Danielle and Christal wandered aimlessly to the edge of the parking lot, but no one followed. They moved back toward the crowd. A fireman came and put a sheet around Danielle and Ethan. His gesture of kindness almost unraveled Danielle. She desperately wanted to cling to his strong arms so his embrace could impart strength to her, but instead she thanked him before he quietly and dutifully moved along. The two women then carried the children across the street and into an empty parking lot.

"Those clouds are circling back," Christal warned.

Could another tornado hit us? Wasn't this one enough? thought Danielle.

There was no place to hide except under a bent-over light pole. God would have to protect Andrew in the gas-leaking hospital and Danielle in the exposed outdoors if things were about to get worse.

From the other side of the street, Christal faintly heard an announcement for people with children to come to where a small truck with an extended cab was waiting to drive them to safety. It all seemed so organized. Danielle didn't want to miss the ride. She ran ahead to reserve their place while Christal followed with Emily.

Everyone was loaded before Danielle and Christal got there.

"Kids in the cab. Parents in the bed." Someone took charge.

"No, I'm not leaving them," Danielle resisted.

What if another tornado came? she thought. *They would have to be in my arms for me to protect them.*

Danielle sat Ethan on the seat and leapt headfirst over the bewildered children to get to the backseat. She then pulled her children over the seatback in front of her and held them in her lap. Christal compliantly got in the bed, and they were taken to a small brick building and ushered inside.

People were congregating at the entrance, smoking, so Danielle led the way down the steps to a small hallway with chairs facing open offices. A man came and offered them water. They accepted.

A few silent minutes passed before someone yelled from the entrance, "This building is not structurally sound!"

Nothing else had to be said. They dashed up the stairs and out again into the smoke-filled drizzly rain. A van came by to help transport people. Everyone was to go to Freeman Hospital and meet in the entryway. Christal and Danielle were ushered out first. The van already held a family of six. Their shelter had been the drive-thru at the bank, and they were numb.

Three people sat in the backseat, and two were in the front. A rear-facing infant seat was in the middle between Danielle and Christal. Danielle looked into the little boy's face, and her eyes began to moisten. This family had made it, too, and now they were selflessly serving those without means of transportation.

13

August and September

Numbness seems to accompany survival. It's hard to do the work of grieving or even feel anything some days. The work of living drowns out the work of healing. I spent the summer mostly trying to do what was required of me. Delight and depression were both muted, even though they were both present. I needed to come to a place where I could accept the sorrow and release its grip on me.

Like waves lapping onto the beach, acceptance and the wholeness it brings did sweep over me at times. Only a few weeks after leaving Joplin, I sat in bed next to Andrew as we wrestled with future plans. I realized that our life, the whole of our experience in Joplin, was gone. Even if we did move back, things would be new. We'd start new routines in new places, and we'd be different. We couldn't go back in time, nor pretend moving back to Joplin would replace what we lost. Accepting that reality released me from trying to re-create life and enabled me to embrace the life I now had. Some of my pain washed away that day.

Months later, I was sitting in church next to Andrew. We were actually early enough to help our reluctant kids go to class and escape in time to hear some of the song service. "On a hill, far away, stood an old rugged cross ..."

I smiled. It was Andrew's favorite hymn. I could almost imagine him as a young boy standing in his small town church belting out the words with passion on his face. I thought of that church and the good times we'd had together there with his family. With his grandpa and grandma. They were gone. It hit me. I felt small as I sat and cried. It was easier to imagine they were still in their house in Kansas, and we just hadn't taken the time to visit or call than it was to wrestle with the reality that they were gone. Yet accepting that reality let the waves wash over me again, and I felt more complete.

In September, I attended a women's conference at my childhood summer campground. The speaker this year was an acquaintance of mine from Joplin. The chance to meet more women intrigued me, and I was desperate for a connection with someone who was experiencing the healing in Joplin firsthand. When I got there, more than I expected was waiting for me.

Worship touches a part of us that nothing else can. It's a deep place inside us where we hold our most precious emotions. And as we sang that morning, I found my heart flooded inside me. The words of every song painted pictures in my mind and tears I had been too busy to allow now poured freely down my face. I began reliving, scene by scene, our drive to the hospital, the fear of being locked out, and the terror of the wind around me. And then a new song was sung.

It was a song I'd never heard before. The melody was in beautiful contrast to what was flashing in my mind, and as I listened to the words, the two melded together. The lyrics spoke of God singing over me, echoing Zephaniah 3:17, "The LORD your God is with you, he is mighty to save. He will take great delight in you, he will quiet you with his love, he will rejoice over you with singing." I saw myself again huddled down on the cold hospital floor with Ethan under me. Glass was breaking all around me, and I was singing. The picture changed, like a camera zooming out, and it was as if I could see the unseen. As I sang to my child, the Lord Almighty covered me and sang to his.

14

Sunday, May 22nd

Approximately 6:30 p.m.

Andrew was evacuated from the hospital not long after Danielle left it. Seeing the devastation for the first time was, to his mind, like the shock that the cold, wet air was to his skin. He shivered in the wheelchair, with the oxygen mask over his nose and mouth. He wondered how big the storm had been, and he was feeling certain his house was hit.

A lady with arms full of blankets came and put one over his shoulders, one on his lap, and one over his head as more rain began to fall. His heart swelled with thankfulness at her simple, caring gesture.

He was moved farther into the rain to escape the leaking gas pouring out of the hospital, and as he waited, he kept trying his phone in hopes of making contact with family. No one knew they had survived.

Volunteers were starting to arrive, and as the crowd swelled, Andrew saw a familiar face. One of his classmates, who had also gotten her nursing degree the previous day, had come with her husband to help however they could. His ribs hurt as his voice rose, but the need for a familiar connection outweighed the momentary pain.

"Lauren. LAUREN." She finally heard him calling out and came over.

"Andrew! What are you doing here? Were you working today?"

"No. We came here to seek shelter. I'm pretty sure I have a few broken ribs, but Danielle and the kids are okay."

This was Andrew's first brief chance to articulate his experiences. He felt more like a person than a victim at that moment, which gave him hope.

The patients who had been in the psychiatric ward were easy to spot in their hospital-issued scrubs.

Everyone was being prodded to move farther away from the building, and as Andrew passed their group, he overheard one patient bumming a cigarette and attempting to light up before everyone in hearing distance quickly chastised him for putting them all in danger. Smoking around a gas leak could have been disastrous, but after what they'd already experienced, in their relief at a crisis averted, it became a humorous moment.

After sitting alone for some time, Andrew was relieved to see his classmate again. She and her husband had agreed to use their truck to help relocate the injured and offered to take Andrew and the nurse who was caring for him. The traffic was thick as they made their way to Memorial Hall, which had been quickly converted into a makeshift emergency room.

As their car came into range of an operating cell tower, Andrew's phone flooded with missed calls, texts, and voice mails. At this point, his battery was almost worn down, but before it died, he got out these words to their family, "We 4 are okay."

For the past hour, Danielle's parents, stuck in a hotel room sixty miles outside of Joplin, paced the room. They knew Dalenna was safe and Andrew and Danielle had been at St. John's. The news was of no comfort. Their daughter was last known to be headed toward the most iconic image of destruction being flashed on their TV screen.

Diana called her mama.

"Mama, I'm so worried. We haven't heard from Danielle and Andrew yet. I don't think they made it."

As she poured out her fears, tears streamed down her face. Mothers and daughters are curious things, especially when those daughters are mothers as well. Diana's mother was concerned and worried for her granddaughter and great-grandchildren, but she was also concerned for her daughter who was crumbling under the weight of her anguish. She knew Diana could be strong for Danielle, but in this moment, she was falling apart. The words that came surprised her daughter, but it gave her what she needed.

"Have faith, Diana!" came a strong, rebuking voice on the other end of the line.

Like a splash of cold water in her face, Diana sat up straight with renewed strength to wait and trust the Lord. She didn't have to wait long. Andrew's delightful text soon came bearing those beautiful words, "We 4 are okay." She and Dale hugged, cried, fell on their knees next to their hotel room bed, and thanked the Lord.

15

Sunday, May 22nd

Approximately 7:30 p.m.

Andrew walked into Memorial Hall and immediately remembered coming here for a concert with Danielle about ten years earlier, before they were even dating. Where booths of merchandise had been set up for people to mill around before and after the show was now a reception area for patients.

"Name and date of birth, please."

Andrew complied, but his head was spinning from standing. A handwritten slip of paper was passed to him to be used as his ID tag. His eyes started to go out of focus, and before he knew it, he was guided to lie down on the floor with his feet on a nearby chair. A doctor Andrew recognized came to check on him. He remembered Andrew and thoroughly assessed him. Glass had wedged itself into the skin on Andrew's back, which the doctor gently removed. There were no pain medications available for anyone, but workers did their best to comfort the injured.

In order to move Andrew inside the concert hall with the other patients, a backboard was brought, and six people were assembled. They rolled him to his right side and quickly slipped the board under him as he screamed in agony. His right side was where he had directly crashed into the door frame.

Soon he found himself lying on a table, staring at the ceiling while a volunteer stood by his side holding his IV bag. There were no IV poles, so for every person who needed an IV, another person was needed to hold it.

So many people were in pain. The room was a cacophony of moans and echoing voices, which were drowned out by intermittent screams of pain. With limited supplies, the available staff was restricted to giving fluids and offering rudimentary care.

Help was on the way. Ambulances came from surrounding communities, some from hours away, ready to evacuate people. Critical patients first. Helicopters were ready, shuttling patients quickly to hospitals that could handle the care.

When it was Andrew's turn to be moved, the entire table he was on was picked up and moved outside. He could hear his situation being debated. A helicopter had returned and could be used again. He was almost loaded there. Childish excitement was building, but another patient had a greater need. So it was decided that Andrew would share an ambulance from Little Rock, Arkansas, that was on its way to Pittsburg, Kansas.

He was rolled to his left side, per his request, and another backboard transferred him to the ambulance bed. Getting Andrew loaded beside the other patient proved a bit of a challenge. As tall as he was, his feet kept sticking out the door. After several attempts, the EMTs finally jockeyed his bed into a position that would allow the doors to be closed, and away they went.

At the hospital, his favorite jeans and nice red polo shirt were cut off him. The only items spared were his shoes and belt. A full body CT scan was ordered, and finally, he got pain medicines. With neither broken bones nor head trauma, he was free to go.

His sister, Elizabeth, came into the room with teary-eyed relief showing on her face. It had been a hard night for her, waiting for news, praying, and wishing she could do something to help. It was late in the evening when she had received a text from Danielle's sister, Dalenna. The nurse riding with Andrew in the ambulance had called Dalenna to update the family on Andrew's stable condition and location. Since Elizabeth was the closest family member to the hospital, she was asked to meet Andrew and bring him what he would need.

With a task at hand, she had scrambled through her house looking for clothes. Her brother was at least two sizes larger than she and her husband, but she eventually found a pair of Andrew's old high school shorts and the only XL shirt in the house. She gave the clothes to Andrew, who immediately started laughing. The shirt's logo had a large tornado with eyes and comical boxing gloves on the front. In their family's odd sense of humor, it was perfect. He slipped his shoes back on over the provided hospital socks, and they left.

16

Sunday, May 22nd

Approximately 7:30 p.m.

Sitting on a small bench in Freeman Hospital, Danielle and her children waited. She was certain Andrew would come in the front doors at any minute. As they sat, the shock started to wear off. Here, not even one mile from St. John's Hospital, everything was clean, organized, and whole. It was in stark contrast to everything else they had seen since 5:40 p.m. Ethan woke out of his dreamlike trance and began to act like the curious, playful little boy he usually was. While

Ethan became more engaged, Emily clung tightly to Danielle and disappeared more into herself, emerging only briefly when a nurse came over and asked, "Would your kids like a juice?" Danielle nodded as the nurse leaned over and whispered apologetically, "I don't have enough to give them each one. Can they share?" Danielle nodded with a smile and gratefully accepted. Emily sat up, momentarily excited about the new treasure that had just arrived. Juice was a treat and a tangible indicator that normal life and good things were going to happen again.

A small woman in her fifties came and sat near Danielle. She was obviously shaken up and needed to tell her story. "We were in our house. It's all gone now. The whole house, but we made it. My husband was admitted because he needs his meds, but we weren't really hurt," she paused and then continued. "It's all gone. We just built a new deck and put in an above ground pool. Finished it this afternoon. Look, I have a picture of it on my phone. Can you believe it? It completely blew away. I don't know what I'm going to do tonight. I can't call anyone. My cell phone won't connect at all."

"You are welcome to stay with us," Danielle immediately offered.

"Where's your house?"

"Just a couple blocks south of the high school." Noticing a peculiar look on her new acquaintance's face, she added, "Why?"

"You might not have a house either. I heard the high school is basically gone."

The path of the storm was much larger than Danielle realized. Stretching from west to east was a path of destruction that affected one-third of the city. It's odd what came to mind in those moments. *If our house was hit, then I don't have a place to stay tonight either. Oh no...I left that little plastic lawn mower out in the backyard. The kids loved that. I'm sure it's gone.* Other families were mourning similarly trivial things. Danielle overheard a family lament that they had just put pancakes away in the fridge for breakfast tomorrow. They had escaped with only the clothes on their backs.

As Danielle sat and waited to be rescued, Emily began to complain of her eye hurting. Danielle was worried about Emily, which was a feeling that would persist over the next six months or more. Emily remembered the noise, her daddy holding her, the wind, and Christal carrying her. The world was a scary place in this little girl's eyes, but healing would come to her, too.

When another nurse came by to see if they needed anything, Danielle asked her to take a look at Emily, especially her eye. The nurse escorted them to the pediatric ward where Emily was briefly checked over, and her eye was flushed. Once the debris was washed away, Emily felt much better. It was less chaotic here, but Danielle feared Andrew wouldn't be able to find them now.

They were given blankets, and since it was already 8:30 and bedtime for the little ones, Danielle was led to the ward's playroom. She made a bed out of a bench and a chair and sang her little ones to sleep while lights from rescue vehicles flashed through the window.

Thankful to be in a warm, safe place, Danielle was now very aware of her isolation. When one of the nurses asked if she needed anything, the first thing in her mind was letting her family know they had survived and where they were now located.

"Do you have a working cell that I could use?"

"Calls aren't going through, but I've been able to send a few text messages. You can try it," the nurse offered.

Just a week ago, while driving to church, Danielle decided to memorize her parents' cell phone numbers. She had been thinking back to her childhood and how, at that time, she knew the number for anyone she called frequently. Feeling too dependent on her cell, she put the most important numbers to memory.

Thankful for that premonition, she was able to contact her parents and sister. Dalenna was staying the night at John's father's house where her phone had good reception, so she was able to get the word out immediately to Andrew's parents and sister. After corresponding with them, she wrote back to Danielle, "Pamela [Andrew's mom] is at Freeman and can help with the kids."

That text was much better news than Dalenna realized. Andrew's parents were alive. Pamela wouldn't have been available to help with the children if her husband hadn't made it. They had not been swept away in the tornado as Andrew thought.

Karl and Pamela found Danielle and told their story. They had ridden out the storm in their bathtub, which was what Karl wanted to tell Andrew on the phone, "It's too late for us … too late to come to the hospital." Just one street away, the tornado damaged several homes, but their house was spared. They could all spend the night there even though it had no power.

After climbing out of their tub and seeing the damage nearby, Karl and Pamela drove to Andrew and

Danielle's house, only coming to the hospital after they realized it was empty. Karl, a nurse, did what he could to help. When he was free, the five of them walked out together as the day came to a close.

May 22, 2011, ended very differently than it had begun. In a blink, everything changed. None of the petty details, so important in the morning, mattered that night. Life would, from this moment on, be different. Most days begin and end similarly, but anyone who's been in an accident, been diagnosed with a life-threatening illness, or lost something that seemed secure knows that perspective changes in that moment. It's a gift, but not one you'd wish on anyone. It calls to us to appreciate what matters, to see beyond the mundane and to long for the eternal. As May 23 dawned, a new path had been placed before the Stammers, and walking down it would change them for the better.

17

October

In a blink, the summer was gone, and autumn had come. I felt a little cheated. I love summer, and I missed it. I expected time would stand still until I had gotten back on my feet, and then we would move forward together. Autumn came as a wake-up call. It made me sad to see the dying part of the year come when I was just starting to live again. New growth, flowers blooming, and warm sun, that's the picture I wanted to see.

Looking back, autumn became a perfect description of where I was. As the seasons were circling to a close,

I realized a chapter of my life was, too. Something had been happening in me while the days shortened and the temperatures dipped lower. I decided to glance back.

A few days after the tornado, all I could see were my plans and how they were taken away from me. I had hope, but it was disciplined hope mixed with shock at all the change. May 25, 2011, read:

> *The last several years have been hard. We moved four times, transitioned, changed our life plans, and survived a rigorous nursing program. We thought we would settle into Andrew's job routine and just try to breathe for a bit, but we now have to figure out how to rebuild our lives, where to live in the meantime, and where Andrew can work, but God is good! "A righteous man may have many troubles, but the Lord delivers him from them all (Psalm 34:19)."*

A month in, I was wavering between deadened and exploding emotions. On June 6, 2011, I wrote:

> *I still feel like I'm glassy-eyed, moving through life in a haze. I'm guessing I had to function on adrenaline for a week or more, and now nothing is urgent. I'm barely even trying to maintain the status quo in my responsibilities. I just don't have the fight in me to push through and get it done. I'm numb.*

The next day, June 7, 2011, I wrote:

I just want to scream. I have almost no time alone.
Things are still out of control, although getting better.
I am exhausted. Having the kids all day, no morning
naps for Ethan, with no car is challenging, and I keep
staying up too late because I'm searching for something,
but watching another new movie isn't fulfilling me.
I want real rest. Lord, I'm running on empty, and I
need you.

Two months in, I was learning how to grieve and how
to dream again. On July 23, 2011, I wrote:

So many things have happened since I last wrote. A
friend called to see how we were doing after he heard
that Grandpa and Grandma Stammer died. He gave us
an opportunity to talk about all that's been going on,
and he gave us some insight from his experiences. He
said that, even though accepting the truth hurt worse
up front, it brought better and quicker healing in the
long run. So, I'm being honest with myself. We lost our
home and our pattern of life, my weekly meeting with
other moms, our library routine, our favorite park, and
our favorite grocery store. We lost our pediatrician,
our garden, and our relaxing summer plans. We lost
some freedom and anonymity, along with our table,

couch, walls, floors, and home. Our flowers, herbs, shed, and swing set are gone. We lost our church family, restaurants, and familiarity. Andrew lost his job at a place where he was really excited about working. We lost our van. We lost a sense of routine and security. After thinking through all this, Andrew and I went on a date. We sat outside over a vineyard, and we talked about our family goals. We feel convinced that our marriage and children are our biggest priorities for the next twenty-five years.

Four months after the tornado, I was becoming a different person. On September 15, 2011, I wrote:

Two nights ago, Andrew and I had a talk. He said he's been praying for me to see the bright side of things again. I've been dwelling on the difficult, frustrating, and negative. I felt loved by what he said and how he said it. I realized I was having a hard time balancing thankfulness and grief, especially when I talk to people. I want them to understand I'm hurting, numb, and bogged down by everything, and that I miss what I lost, and it's hard. So many people remind me of the bright side that I've become increasingly negative in hopes someone will give voice to my pain, but in doing so, I've only hurt myself and my family. I realized I really

just want an excuse for my selfishness. I want to be the
center of attention and pity, and I want to be excused
from lack of interest in anyone else's problems. I needed
to hear what Andrew told me, and I do have so much
to be thankful for, even in the midst of grief.

Then in October, I realized I had already begun to rebuild some of my losses. I joined a new group of mothers who met weekly for encouragement, and I'd chosen a pediatrician. We found a park we liked to play at on warm days. I knew the library events and the bookstore's kids' programming. Our family had several new favorite restaurants. I had a new routine and a new-to-us van, and Andrew had a new job he was excited about.

On a warm evening early in October, we found ourselves standing in the backyard of a new friend's house. We had joined a small group at church, and we were meeting together for the second time. The kids were having a blast running and sliding and playing together, while Andrew and I were able to share some of our story with an interested couple.

Soon squabbles from the sandbox interrupted our conversation. Someone had thrown sand, and a mini-war had erupted with casualties on both sides. I picked up Ethan and realized sand had worked its way through his light hair and was covering his head. I first thought, *This is going to be tough to clean out tonight.* And then like warmth spreading over me, I remembered so many months ago when sand in my hair and ears was a tangible reminder of a trauma I wanted to forget.

The sand on my little boy was evidence of play and new life. Somewhere along the way, that painful, debris-filled grit had all washed away, and I had since forgotten how it had plagued me. The wound in my heart that was then bleeding had scabbed over every time I picked at it, and it was now only a scar, a reminder, no longer hurting, though its mark would always remain. I am a different person than I was on May 22, 2011. That grit on my head was the beginning of a healing process that would leave me stronger, and even if I could go back in time, I wouldn't change a thing.

"The LORD your God is with you, he is mighty to save. He will take great delight in you, he will quiet you with his love, he will rejoice over you with singing."

Zephaniah 3:17

CPSIA information can be obtained at www.ICGtesting.com
Printed in the USA
LVOW080533090512

280979LV00001B/4/P